WEaving HeARTS

Where Emotions Entangle and Hearts Connect

Navisha Deepak Kothari

BookLeaf Publishing

India | USA | UK

Made with ❤ on the BookLeaf Publishing Platform
www.bookleafpub.in
www.bookleafpub.com

Dedication

I dedicate this book to my Mom, dad, and brother, whose unwavering belief in me never faltered. They always held onto the hope that I would one day accomplish something amazing, and this book is a testament to their faith.

To my dear friends—Mehul, Phalguni, and Aditiya—who have been my pillars of support, constantly pushing me forward and standing by me through my lowest moments. Your encouragement has been invaluable.

I also owe a debt of gratitude to my English teacher, Gaurav Sir, whose early guidance ignited my passion for writing and helped me discover my talent many years ago. Your belief in me has made all the difference.

Lastly, to everyone who has been an integral part of my journey—your presence and influence have shaped who I am today. This book is for all of you.

Preface

This book is a reflection of the many emotions I have experienced throughout my journey. It is a collection of poems, each one dedicated to my loved ones and the myriad emotions we all feel as we navigate the complex path called life. Life is not just a journey but a tapestry woven with moments of joy, sorrow, love, and growth— and this book aims to capture those moments in words.

We all weave hearts in the journey of life, forming bonds and creating memories that shape who we are. As I share these poems, I am not just presenting my own experiences; I am offering a mirror, hoping that you will see yourself in these words. These poems are a reflection of the universal emotions that connect us all, reminding us that we are not alone in the struggles and triumphs we face.

Every phase of life brings with it its own set of challenges, triumphs, and transformations. This book encompasses those phases—those feelings and experiences that we all go through in one form or another. I have poured my heart into these verses, with the hope that they resonate with you, just as they have resonated with me in my own journey.

As you read through these poems, I invite you to look beyond the words and see the emotions, the bonds, and the experiences that unite us all. This is not just my story, but a reflection of yours as well. My wish is that, in some way, these poems will help you reflect on your own life, your own journey, and the hearts you've woven along the way.

Acknowledgements

A heartfelt thank you to Vinyasa Earth, the place and the people that helped me remove the blockages I had within myself. I truly believe I would not have embarked on this journey without being at Vinyasa, and without Aayushi's timely writer's challenge that sparked my inspiration to write these poems. To the incredible community that became a second family, offering support, love, and encouragement—your presence in my life has been invaluable. You have created a space that feels like home away from home, and for that, I am forever grateful.

Thank you.

1. New Beginnings

Just at the moment lights got dim
He looked at me, I looked at me
Felt like one whose touch could give me shivers
Still when he touches my heart trembles
The distance from knowing each other
To spending every evening together
Does it really feels this way?
Just want to ask him to stay a bit longer!
Some days, Some celebrations
Some birthday's and New Year's for sure
It's too fast to describe
Still I am sorting what being together would be like
But want to tell him every heart break
Even the first time,
I saw my dad in pain
Need to tell him the time,
I cried alone in night
Even the birthday surprise,
when my mom hugged me tight
I wanna tell him the time,

I thought I would never find anyone
To now, when I found you,
WHO MIGHT BE SOMEONE
So, stay a bit longer
Let's figure out what memories
WE CAN CREATE TOGETHER.....

2. Strength- FATHER

He is the reason for my existence
The person behind my persistence
Says he and me are alike
I am the shadow of his personality so divine

He is the reason for my strength
The person because of whom I stand
Firm and stick to my beliefs
I am the light with which he only sticks

He is the reason for my smile
The person with whose presence sadness can never
become a pile
Happening and chill to be around
With him only the happiness I found

क्यूँ कहते हैं सब वो संभाल लेंगे,
पापा हैं ना, वो हर परेशानी मिटा देंगे,
क्यूँ नहीं हक़ उन्हें कमज़ोर होने का,
आज कहती हूं मुझे गर्व हैं मेरे पापा कि बेटी होने का !!

3. When god made you my MOTHER

जब ख़ुदा ने तुझे मेरे लिए बनाया होगा
उसके मन में मेरा ही तो ख्याल आया होगा
जब देगी जन्म तु मुझे
सर-आंखों और अपने साए में रखेगी सदा मुझे

तु मेरा सहारा है
जैसा तुझसे माँगा तूने वैसा दिया है
तु मेरी शक्ति है
जब जहां जरुरत हुई हमेशा मेरे साथ खड़ी हुई है
जब मैंने चलना सीखा
अकेले दूर जाने का हक़ माँगा
ना मेरे क़दमों को कभी रोका
मेरे उड़ने के लिए कहां तूने है पूरा असमान मेरा
आज भी जब लड़खड़ाती हूं
पीछे मुड़ फिर तेरा साथ पाती हूं

अगर कभी ख़ुदा मुझे भी इस लायक समझे
कोशिश होगी हमेशा मेरी कि तुझ सी चाहत मेरी ममता में भी झलके
ताउम्र तेरी शुक्रगुज़ार रहूंगी

माँ, कहीं भी चली जाऊ, हमेशा तेरी ही लाड़ली रहूंगी !!

कुछ खास धुंध रही थी बड़े होने के बाद
दर्द कि वो दवा दिल टूटने के बाद
एहसास जो सिर्फ तेरे आंचल में है
माँ, तेरे जैसा प्यार कहां पाऊंगी तुझसे दूर होने के बाद !!

4. My First Friend- MY BROTHER

है सच की तेरी बहन हू मै,
पर मेरा पहला दोस्त है तु,
हमराही, हमसफ़र,
इन नामों से तुझे भी पुकार सकती हूं,
मेरे मायके कि हर पल वाली याद होगा तु,
जब याद करू मायका तो माँ नहीं याद आएगा तू,

भाई नहीं तू मेरी जान है,
बचपन से जिससे लड़ी वो याद है,
जवानी में जिसने गलतियां समझाई वो आइना है,
हर बार जिसके कंधे पर रोई वो सहारा है,
तु सिर्फ भाई नहीं मेरा पेहला दोस्त है,

ज़िक्र तेरा जब भी होगा,
चाहे फैसला कितना भी होगा,
हमेशा मेरी मुस्कराहट का कारण बनेगा,
भाई तु ही तो forever वाला रिश्ता होगा,
हू शामिल मै भी तेरी पहचान में,
हम अलग सही लेकिन दिल से हमेशा साथ में !!

5. मेरी सबसे प्यारी सहेली

ए ख़ुदा क्या खूब तूने उसे बनाया है,

जिसने मुझे फ़िर मुस्कुराना सिखाया है,

तौफे तो खूब मिले इस ज़िंदगी में मुझे.

लेक़िन उस जैसी शख्सियत ना थी जीवन में मेरे,

ता-उम्र भी वो साथ रहे तो कम होगा,

ये साथ इस ज़िंदगी में नहीं मुझे हर जन्म में चाहिए होगा,

मेरी परछाई सी लगी वो मेरे दिल को,

ना कोई गुस्सा टिक पता जब भी साथ पाऊ उसको,

दुख से कोसो दूर ले आई है

है साथ वो तो ना कोई और दोस्ती की जरूरत है

सब्दो में पूरी तरह कभी बायां ना कर सकूंगी,

कुछ ऐसी अपनी यारी है!!

6. Dosti

To all the people in my life,
The ones who were there
The ones who felt that I was the best part
The ones who loved me
The ones who left me and
Especially the ones who gave me pain
Thank you for being there
Thank you for teaching me how to grow
Thank you for making me learn
Thank you for making me see things differently
But, most importantly, thank you for coming into my life
Because of the laugh, the pain the hurt
Your entrance all exit in my life gave me
That made me who I am today
That made me strong
That made me capable
Of going through the worst and
still become the best
It might be a happy start,
a rough way,

a roller coaster ride
or a horrifying end
It's because of the past experiences
which made me who I am today
And whether at times I agree or not but I do love myself
and I will always do
Sometimes I miss you
Sometimes I just want bad memories to disappear
But there is no escape
Sooner or later,
I would have to accept what has happened
So, to start the new phase of my life
I want to say goodbye to every past
and every person Who has left my life

7. फिर मुलाक़ात होगी कभी

कुछ यु मिली थी उससे
जैसे नहीं मुलाकात हुई थी किसी से
जब वो लेकर आया ख़ुशियो कि चाबी
सुकून है कि कुछ शामें उसके साथ मिली
पर अब हुए है अलग हम
कि थम गए है मेरे ये कदम
बस उमीद है तो इतनी सी
कि फिर मुलाक़ात होगी कभी

बिताए थे लम्हे कुछ साथ
याद आएगी बीती हर बात
रास्ते हुए जो अब अलग
मंजिल जो एक थी,
वो हुई है अब ख़तम
कुछ समय कि कहानियों को लेकर
आज लड़ रहे है उन्हीं बातों को लेकर
बस उमीद है जब लड़ाइयों कि वज़ह खतम होगी
उस दिन फिर मुलाक़ात होगी

तोड़कर ये जो नाता अलग हुए है

अपनी-अपनी मंजिल कि ओर कदम बढ़ चुके है
ना होंगे अब साथ
ना ख़ुशी और दुख में थामेंगे हाथ
जो यु अब जुदा हुए है
कि अब हम तन्हा हुए है
बस उमीद है fo इतनी सी
कि फिर मुलाक़ात होगी कभी

कभी कीसी मोड पर फिर टकराएँगे
साथ बिताए वो लम्हे याद आएँगे
तो क्या हुआ हम तब अंजान होंगे
फिर किसी मंजिल पर साथ चलेंगे
इस बार कुछ दूर नहीं
उस वक़्त के लिए हमेशा के लिए होगा बस वही
बस ख्वाइश है तो इतनी सी
क़ाश फिर मुलाक़त हो कभी

8. Incomplete Dreams

सपने ये जो तू बुनता है
यूं जो तू ख़ामोश रहता है
हर दिन तेरा जो तू यूं जीता है
ए दिल क्यू तु सबसे दूर रहता है
उड़ता रहता है जो तु यूं आसमां के तले
ज़मीं पर तो तु कभी ना ठहरे
ठहरा जो नहीं तेरा मन है
कैसे रहेगा तु हमेशा खुश
ये बहुत बड़ा किस्सा है
पंखो के साथ भी ठहराव आएगा
किसी ना किसी दिन तु भी घर को वापिस लौट जाएगा
जब याद आएगी इस शाम की
तो चेहरा पर हलकी सी मुस्कान पाएगा
दिल के इन रिश्तों में
कभी मीठे कभी खट्टे इन रिश्तों में
तुझे एहमियत तो जरूर समझ आएगी
हवाओं की महक़ में जो ये खुशबू है
खुशबू जो कभी महसूस ना हुई
दिल जो ये आज भी बेताब है
कोई ना कोई तो ना पुरे होने वाला इसमें ख्वाब है

9. उसूलों की किताब

ए जहान के उसूल लिखने वालो
तुम्हारी किताब में क्या है वजूद उसका
तुम खुद को संस्कारी कहते हो
तो सुनो....बेशर्म है नाम उसका
इस उसूल की किताब से मिलना कुछ है नहीं
तुम्हारे कारण उसने अपनी कितनी ख्वाहिश तिजोरी में बंद है करी हुई
संजोए वो ख्वाब तुमसे पूछकर तो नहीं
फिर क्यों तुमने उनके पूरा होने की चाह छुपा दी है
वो तो एक मासूम के दिल की आरजू है
उस लड़की की जो तुम्हारी चौखट की शान थी
क्यों उस से नजाकत तुमने छीन ली है
क्या उसने तुम्हे अपना सब कुछ मान कर गलती की थी
हा तो उसकी चाह बेबाक थी
पर हर रात मांगी तो उसने तुमसे अपनी खुशी ही थी
जब तुम्हे है शिकायत उस से
तो उसे भी अब मोहब्बत नहीं
जब लकीर खींची है तूने अपनी
मोहब्बत की ताकत से
वो उसे अब मंजूर नहीं
अब चाहो तो तुम उसे भी जलील कर लो

क्यों कि अब उसे तुम्हारा ऐतबार नहीं
बनेगी वो भी एक मिसाल क्यों कि तुम्हारे बनाए उन उसूलों कि
दीवार उसके ख्वाबों से अब कुछ छोटी है
तुम्हारे लिए चाहे ना होगा कुछ वजूद उसका
लेकिन खुदा ने भी सोचकर बनाया है
तकदीर का लिखा ना कोई मिटा पाया है
वो नहीं उन आम लोगों की कदर में
जो छोड़ गए पंछी-ए-ख्वाब को राह में
ताकि वो फिर जन्म ना ले ले
ताकि साथ रहकर उसका गला न घोंटना पड़े
वो है तन्हा ,वो है जादू की पुड़िया
एक पंछी जिसे तुम कैद न कर सकोगे
बेबाक है उसकी शख्सियत तुम्हारी नजरों में
जो मोहब्बत-ए-आसमान में उड़ती हो
उसे क्या ही मद-ए-नजर रखना
जमीन पर पनप रहे बैर से
तुम चाहे कोसों उसे
ना कभी बदस्तूर होने वाली कमीज़ है
वो तो इतराता हुआ रेशम का दुपट्टा है
चाहे कितनी भी कामियाब क्यों ना हो जाए
तुम्हारे मुताबिक़ तो बस वो एक तबाही की पहल है
लफ्जों में तुम कुछ भी शक़्कर घोल कर बोलो
वाक़िफ है वो तुम्हारे लिए बेशरम है
इक बात फिर सुनलो देहलीज को जो ना पार करने दोगे
आफ़त मचा देगी, वो अपने ख्वाबों की रानी हे

10. I am WORTHY!

मासूमियत, नज़ाकत, एहतराम था जब मै बच्चा था
ना दुनिया का ख़ौफ़,
ना हारने-जीतने का ड़र,
बस अपने में ही मग्न था
उम्र बढ़ी, नए लोग ज़िंदगी में आए
कुछ ने अच्छे तो कुछ ने भयानक दृश्य दिखाए
बच्चा अब भी था,
समझ कुछ तब भी कहा आ रहा था
जज़्बात को शब्द देना सिख रहा था
मै तो अकेलेपन और तन्हाई में कहीं गुम हो गया था
बढ़ते बढ़ते घाव कुछ ज्यदा गहरा हो गए
वो बिना सोचे करने के हिस्से कहीं खो गए
बच्चे से लड़कपन कि उम्र में क़दम रखा
फ़िर जो हुआ उस पर ग़ौर करना छोड़ दिया था
बस सोचा दर्द को भुला कर आज में ज़ी लू
ये कड़वी यादों का जिक्र क्यों ही किसी से करू
लेकिन वो किस्से आज में भी अपना असर दिखा रहे थे
वो साऐ की तरह मेरे साथ ही तो चल रहे थे
चलते चलते कुछ छाव नजर आई
जहां थे मुझ जैसा महसूस करने वाले कई

बात हुई तो नज़र आई उस हिस्से का असर भी
कैसे दिखाई दे रहा था कल मेरे आज में भी
एहसास हुआ टूट कर पंहुचा था जो मै छाव में
साथ ने, सबके विश्वास और मेरे सब्र ने
रास्ता अत्तीत से निकलने का दिखाया मुझे आज में
घर से दूर एक घर जैसा नज़र आया उन में
फ़िर क्या, ड़र से निकल कर उस बच्चे ने अपनी आहट सुनाई
गिर के उठने पर ही मुझे अपनी कद्र समझ आई

11. ड़र - नफ़रत या मोहब्बत

अल्हड़ सी ज़िद्दी सी एक बच्ची
मासूम शक्ल, छोटी आँखे और दिल कि सच्ची
निकली जंग पर हराने उस अकेलेपन के एहसास को
जीने, खुश रहने, नहीं किसी से उमीद अब उसको
खुद कि परछाई से ही लड़ बैठी
गुस्सा अंदर था बहुत, उसे शब्द ना दे पाई बस वो चिल्ला पाती
यूं तो ख़ामोश थी उसके दर्द कि आवाज़
लेकिन फिर भी मोहब्बत थी उस मंजर में
इस ड़र में परेशानी है और आराम भी
जितनी है नफ़रत उसे उतनी है मोहब्बत भी

12. My Heartbeat - Destiny

My fear, my heart, and my heartbeat,
All come together when I feel it,
Heard, seen, and recognized,
Things you might want to leave behind,
Like a kid, playing in sand,
Juggling, enjoying, and being in the moment,
We all forget those tiny parts,
And grow up and struggle in life drama,
Need to break out in tears,
Shout out LOUD,
Scream and move around,
By the end, LIE IN PEACE,
Feeling that it's just destiny played its piece.

13. Waves of Life

इस मंजर पर आकर मदहोश हूं मै
सुकून पाकर खुदमें ही ख़ामोश हूं मै
लहरों मे बहने कि कोशिश करते हुए
बीते लम्हों के एहसास को आज जीते हुए
सब कुछ होते हुए भी कुछ ना होने के गम में
जिंदगी कि भाग-दौड़ में मिलने वाले उस पल में
नया कुछ तो है हर दिन में
चलो, आज को ही आज़मा कर देखते हैं

14. Silence- The Best Language

What's that language which is understood by all?

A minimal gesture that is often overseen,
Not understood and always undervalued by us all,
What if we look inside,
And see what we all have been leaving behind,
The anger that steals everything from you,
Relations would become strong if we stay quiet for a
minute or few,
Being quiet for a single second,
Isn't it better than fighting for a million minutes,
Being silent is also a way to apologize,
If we remain silent, it means we realize,
Introspection for a second will save us from destroying
many bonds!!

15. Destiny: Choice or Chance

Destiny is a choice or by chance,
We can identify it by having a glance,
By chance, we can see it in every case,
Where a person loses or wins in a second space,
Choice is what we are doing,
Our hard work does give us something,
Some say everything that will happen is written,
But how can any god give us something we didn't do
efforts for?
If we think it could be true,
No one would do the work that he doesn't want to do
But everything depends on us
We should do only what our mind says
Do your job and always be truthful,
Only that can make your life meaningful
No destiny can decide your life,
Not by chance, nor by choice.

16. Illusion of Senses

Eyes behold a world so vast,
Yet truth and lies blend so fast.

Ears hear whispers, loud and deep,
But can they catch the pain we keep?

The nose inhales the scents of time,
Memories lost in fragrance divine.

The tongue savors bitter and sweet,
Yet words it spills, cut or heal deep.

Touch can comfort; touch can sting,
A silent echo, a hidden string.

Five senses shape the world we feel,
Yet is it all just the mind's appeal?

What we see may not be true,
What we hear is colored, too.

Perception bends, reality sways,
The mind reshapes in endless ways.

While using all the sense, there is a world unknown
Within the reach of mind yet to be shown.

Here lies the art of focusing on a single sense
diving deep into power each one can comprehend.

17. योग निंद्रा

Eyes are closed, still I can see,
Sky of imagination where my soul can fly free,
Drift away from the external chaos,
Dove into the internal sound that echo's.

Sound that is hard to heard,
Recognizing the power of acceptance it holds,
Leaving external stress and worry behind,
Silence of thoughts and eternal light I find.

Bathing in that light, I found the truth,
In which soul took the flight,
Meeting with the unknown higher self,
Guiding to the purpose of my being,
At last, identifying the motive cleared,
And my inner powers revealed !!

18. The Peace of Poetry

वक़्त को थाम कर हाथों में रख लूं,

इस पल में, ख़ुदको ही मै धुंध लूं,

मदहोश हो गई हूं भागती दौड़ती ज़िंदगी में,

तलाश है उस पल कि जब मन हो सुकून में,

महसूस कर उस पल को पन्ने पर उतार दू,

लिख कर एहसास मन को मै मुक्त करूँ,

बेचैनी का ये है साधन मेरा,

एहसास को शब्द देना ही है सुकून मेरा !!

19. Fear of Breaking Comfort Zone

The zone that I feel safe in
The place that just let's me in
Keeps me calm
Keeps me at ease
Like the baby resting in mother's womb
It is hard to leave without tears or causing pain
But have to step out into the world
See, try, win, loose and become the best self
Without trying we can't grow
Not stepping out of comfort zone
Is just living in the mother's womb forever
Is that what you want or you wanna go out and not let
anything hold you back again?

20. नया स्वरूप

हर पन्ने, हर किस्से, हर कहानी को मोड़ा है,
कोई ना समझ पाएगा उसने ख़ुदको कितना तोड़ा है,
शुरुआत तो कब्कि हो चुकी थी,
अस्लियत तो काफ़ी समय बाद समझ आई थी,
मायूसी और बेबसी यूं रंग लाई थी,
अतीत की तस्वीर जब दीवार पर नज़र आई थी,
छोड़ कर उसे वो यूं आगे बढ़ी है,
हर दुख देने वाले बहाने को भूल चुकी है,
यूं अब वो नए रंग में रंग गई,
तु जो ना पा सकेगा, कुछ ऐसी वो हो गई !!

21. Would I ever be able to love someone?

Everyone in past had flaw
That stopped me from letting the relationship grow
All had Something which made it simple
For me not to regret falling out of love
But.. here I am now.
Wondering how i can i stop loving you
The only wrong you do has a reason
You don't feel the way I do
Still at times you go above and beyond
To make me feel fine
Care attention love and support
No one can wonder how difficult these smallest feelings
are to find
And I have them all with you
There was the reason I falled for you in a day
Everyday I am best version of myself with you, I wanna
say
We support,care and make each other try hard to be
better

Still don't know why we can't be together
You don't want me, that should be enough to make me
walk away
But here I am.. Still longing
For your affection and love
For everything i thought i deserve
I don't know who will be as perfect for me as you
The patience to my chaos
The motivation in the darkness
The happy moment to my dull day
You have been everything
But now you will walk away..
I kissed my number of idiots..
But i was the first in your list
And there is more that you desire but never me
So. I let you walk away, even though,
No one would be as perfect for me as you..
How would i love anyone ever again
When i know my heart has you locked inside..